— MARK —

GOOD NEWS
GOSPEL

THE BIBLE SOCIETIES

Good News New Testament – Second Edition © 1994

Text, illustrations and all helps are copyright
New Testament © American Bible Society 1966, 1971, 1976, 1992
Maps © United Bible Societies 1976, 1978

Title	Code	ISBN
Gospel of Mark	GNB560P MK	0 564 044334

1995/50M(2)
Typeset by BFBS Production Services Department (TP Section)
Printed in Great Britain by HarperCollins *Publishers* Ltd, UK

Quotation Rights for the Good News Bible

Contents

THE GOSPEL ACCORDING TO

MARK

INTRODUCTION

The Gospel according to Mark begins with the statement that it is "the Good News about Jesus Christ, the Son of God". Jesus is pictured as a man of action and authority. His authority is seen in his teaching, in his power over demons, and in forgiving people's sins. Jesus speaks of himself as the Son of Man, who came to give his life to set people free from sin.

Mark presents the story of Jesus in a straightforward, vigorous way, with emphasis on what Jesus did, rather than on his words and teachings. After a brief prologue about John the Baptist and the baptism and temptation of Jesus, the writer immediately takes up Jesus' ministry of healing and teaching. As time goes on, the followers of Jesus come to understand him better, but Jesus' opponents become more hostile. The closing chapters report the events of Jesus' last week of earthly life, especially his crucifixion and resurrection.

The two endings to the Gospel, which are enclosed in brackets, are generally regarded as written by someone other than the author of *Mark*.

Outline of Contents

The Preaching of John the Baptist
(Mt 3.1–12; Lk 3.1–18; Jn 1.19–28)

1 This is the Good News about Jesus Christ, the Son
of God. ᵃ ² It began as the prophet Isaiah had written:
"God said, 'I will send my messenger ahead of you
    to clear the way for you.'
³ Someone is shouting in the desert,
    'Get the road ready for the Lord;
    make a straight path for him to travel!' "

⁴ So John appeared in the desert, baptizing and preaching. ᵇ "Turn away from your sins and be baptized," he told
the people, "and God will forgive your sins." ⁵ Many people
from the province of Judea and the city of Jerusalem went out
to hear John. They confessed their sins, and he baptized them
in the River Jordan.

⁶ John wore clothes made of camel's hair, with a leather
belt round his waist, and his food was locusts and wild honey.
⁷ He announced to the people, "The man who will come after
me is much greater than I am. I am not good enough even to
bend down and untie his sandals. ⁸ I baptize you with water,
but he will baptize you with the Holy Spirit."

The Baptism and Temptation of Jesus
(Mt 3.13—4.11; Lk 3.21–22; 4.1–13)

⁹ Not long afterwards Jesus came from Nazareth in the
province of Galilee, and was baptized by John in the Jordan.

a **1.1** *Some manuscripts do not have* the Son of God.
b **1.4** John appeared in the desert, baptizing and preaching; *some
manuscripts have* John the Baptist appeared in the desert, preaching.

¹⁰ As soon as Jesus came up out of the water, he saw heaven opening and the Spirit coming down on him like a dove. ¹¹ And a voice came from heaven, "You are my own dear Son. I am pleased with you."

¹² At once the Spirit made him go into the desert, ¹³ where he stayed 40 days, being tempted by Satan. Wild animals were there also, but angels came and helped him.

Jesus Calls Four Fishermen
(Mt 4.12–22; Lk 4.14–15; 5.1–11)

¹⁴ After John had been put in prison, Jesus went to Galilee and preached the Good News from God. ¹⁵ "The right time has come," he said, "and the Kingdom of God is near! Turn away from your sins and believe the Good News!"

¹⁶ As Jesus walked along the shore of Lake Galilee, he saw two fishermen, Simon and his brother Andrew, catching fish with a net. ¹⁷ Jesus said to them, "Come with me, and I will teach you to catch people." ¹⁸ At once they left their nets and went with him.

At once they left their nets   (1.18)

¹⁹ He went a little farther on and saw two other brothers, James and John, the sons of Zebedee. They were in their boat getting their nets ready. ²⁰ As soon as Jesus saw them, he called them; they left their father Zebedee in the boat with the hired men and went with Jesus.

A Man with an Evil Spirit
(Lk 4.31–37)

²¹ Jesus and his disciples came to the town of Capernaum, and on the next Sabbath Jesus went to the synagogue and

began to teach. ²² The people who heard him were amazed at the way he taught, for he wasn't like the teachers of the Law; instead, he taught with authority.

²³ Just then a man with an evil spirit in him came into the synagogue and screamed, ²⁴ "What do you want with us, Jesus of Nazareth? Are you here to destroy us? I know who you are — you are God's holy messenger!"

²⁵ Jesus ordered the spirit, "Be quiet, and come out of the man!"

²⁶ The evil spirit shook the man hard, gave a loud scream, and came out of him. ²⁷ The people were all so amazed that they started saying to one another, "What is this? Is it some kind of new teaching? This man has authority to give orders to the evil spirits, and they obey him!"

²⁸ And so the news about Jesus spread quickly everywhere in the province of Galilee.

Jesus Heals Many People
(Mt 8.14–17; Lk 4.38–41)

²⁹ Jesus and his disciples, including James and John, left the synagogue and went straight to the home of Simon and Andrew. ³⁰ Simon's mother-in-law was sick in bed with a fever, and as soon as Jesus arrived, he was told about her. ³¹ He went to her, took her by the hand, and helped her up. The fever left her, and she began to wait on them.

³² After the sun had set and evening had come, people brought to Jesus all the sick and those who had demons. ³³ All the people of the town gathered in front of the house. ³⁴ Jesus healed many who were sick with all kinds of diseases and drove out many demons. He would not let the demons say anything, because they knew who he was.

Jesus Preaches in Galilee
(Lk 4.42–44)

³⁵ Very early the next morning, long before daylight, Jesus got up and left the house. He went out of the town to a lonely place, where he prayed. ³⁶ But Simon and his companions went out searching for him, ³⁷ and when they found him, they said, "Everyone is looking for you."

Took her by the hand, and . . . the fever left her   (1.31)

³⁸ But Jesus answered, "We must go on to the other villages round here. I have to preach in them also, because that is why I came."

³⁹ So he travelled all over Galilee, preaching in the synagogues and driving out demons.

Jesus Heals a Man
(Mt 8.1–4; Lk 5.12–16)

⁴⁰ A man suffering from a dreaded skin disease came to Jesus, knelt down, and begged him for help. "If you want to," he said, "you can make me clean."[a]

⁴¹ Jesus was filled with pity,[b] and stretched out his hand and touched him. "I do want to," he answered. "Be clean!" ⁴² At once the disease left the man, and he was clean. ⁴³ Then Jesus spoke sternly to him and sent him away at once, ⁴⁴ after saying to him, "Listen, don't tell anyone about this. But go

a **1.40** MAKE ME CLEAN: *This disease was considered to make a person ritually unclean.*
b **1.41** pity; *some manuscripts have* anger.

straight to the priest and let him examine you; then in order
to prove to everyone that you are cured, offer the sacrifice
that Moses ordered."

⁴⁵ But the man went away and began to spread the news
everywhere. Indeed, he talked so much that Jesus could not
go into a town publicly. Instead, he stayed out in lonely
places, and people came to him from everywhere.

Jesus Heals a Paralysed Man
(Mt 9.1–8; Lk 5.17–26)

2 A few days later Jesus went back to Capernaum, and the
news spread that he was at home. ² So many people came
together that there was no room left, not even out in front
of the door. Jesus was preaching the message to them ³ when
four men arrived, carrying a paralysed man to Jesus. ⁴ Because of the crowd, however, they could not get the man to
him. So they made a hole in the roof right above the place
where Jesus was. When they had made an opening, they let
the man down, lying on his mat. ⁵ Seeing how much faith
they had, Jesus said to the paralysed man, "My son, your
sins are forgiven."

⁶ Some teachers of the Law who were sitting there
thought to themselves, ⁷ "How does he dare to talk like this?
This is blasphemy! God is the only one who can forgive
sins!"

⁸ At once Jesus knew what they were thinking, so he said
to them, "Why do you think such things? ⁹ Is it easier to say
to this paralysed man, 'Your sins are forgiven', or to say, 'Get
up, pick up your mat, and walk'? ¹⁰ I will prove to you, then,
that the Son of Man has authority on earth to forgive sins."
So he said to the paralysed man, ¹¹ "I tell you, get up, pick
up your mat, and go home!"

¹² While they all watched, the man got up, picked up his
mat, and hurried away. They were all completely amazed and
praised God, saying, "We have never seen anything like this!"

Jesus Calls Levi
(Mt 9.9–13; Lk 5.27–32)

¹³ Jesus went back again to the shore of Lake Galilee.
A crowd came to him, and he started teaching them. ¹⁴ As

he walked along, he saw a tax collector, Levi son of Alphaeus, sitting in his office. Jesus said to him, "Follow me." Levi got up and followed him.

¹⁵ Later on Jesus was having a meal in Levi's house.ᵃ A large number of tax collectors and other outcasts were following Jesus, and many of them joined him and his disciples at the table. ¹⁶ Some teachers of the Law, who were Pharisees, saw that Jesus was eating with these outcasts and tax collectors, so they asked his disciples, "Why does he eat with such people?"

¹⁷ Jesus heard them and answered, "People who are well do not need a doctor, but only those who are sick. I have not come to call respectable people, but outcasts."

The Question about Fasting
(Mt 9.14–17; Lk 5.33–39)

¹⁸ On one occasion the followers of John the Baptist and the Pharisees were fasting. Some people came to Jesus and asked him, "Why is it that the disciples of John the Baptist and the disciples of the Pharisees fast, but yours do not?"

¹⁹ Jesus answered, "Do you expect the guests at a wedding party to go without food? Of course not! As long as the bridegroom is with them, they will not do that. ²⁰ But the day will come when the bridegroom will be taken away from them, and then they will fast.

²¹ "No one uses a piece of new cloth to patch up an old coat, because the new patch will shrink and tear off some of the old cloth, making an even bigger hole. ²² Nor does anyone pour new wine into used wineskins, because the wine will burst the skins, and both the wine and the skins will be ruined. Instead, new wine must be poured into fresh wineskins."

The Question about the Sabbath
(Mt 12.1–8; Lk 6.1–5)

²³ Jesus was walking through some cornfields on the Sabbath. As his disciples walked along with him, they began to pick the ears of corn. ²⁴ So the Pharisees said to Jesus, "Look, it is against our Law for your disciples to do that on the Sabbath!"

a 2.15 in Levi's house; *or* in his *(that is,* Jesus'*)* house.

²⁵ Jesus answered, "Have you never read what David did that time when he needed something to eat? He and his men were hungry, ²⁶ so he went into the house of God and ate the bread offered to God. This happened when Abiathar was the High Priest. According to our Law only the priests may eat this bread — but David ate it and even gave it to his men."

²⁷ And Jesus concluded, "The Sabbath was made for the good of human beings; they were not made for the Sabbath. ²⁸ So the Son of Man is Lord even of the Sabbath."

The Man with a Paralysed Hand
(Mt 12.9–14; Lk 6.6–11)

3 Then Jesus went back to the synagogue, where there was a man who had a paralysed hand. ² Some people were there who wanted to accuse Jesus of doing wrong; so they watched him closely to see whether he would heal the man on the Sabbath. ³ Jesus said to the man, "Come up here to the front." ⁴ Then he asked the people, "What does our Law allow us to do on the Sabbath? To help or to harm? To save someone's life or to destroy it?"

But they did not say a thing. ⁵ Jesus was angry as he looked round at them, but at the same time he felt sorry for them, because they were so stubborn and wrong. Then he said to the man, "Stretch out your hand." He stretched it out, and it became well again. ⁶ So the Pharisees left the synagogue and met at once with some members of Herod's party, and they made plans to kill Jesus.

A Crowd by the Lake

⁷ Jesus and his disciples went away to Lake Galilee, and a large crowd followed him. They had come from Galilee, from Judea, ⁸ from Jerusalem, from the territory of Idumea, from the territory on the east side of the Jordan, and from the region round the cities of Tyre and Sidon. All these people came to Jesus because they had heard of the things he was doing. ⁹ The crowd was so large that Jesus told his disciples to get a boat ready for him, so that the people would not crush him. ¹⁰ He had healed many people, and all those who were ill kept pushing their way to him in order

The crowd was so large   (3.9)

to touch him. ¹¹ And whenever the people who had evil spirits in them saw him, they would fall down before him and scream, "You are the Son of God!"

¹² Jesus sternly ordered the evil spirits not to tell anyone who he was.

Jesus Chooses the Twelve Apostles
(Mt 10.1–4; Lk 6.12–16)

¹³ Then Jesus went up a hill and called to himself the men he wanted. They came to him, ¹⁴ and he chose twelve, whom he named apostles. "I have chosen you to be with me," he told them. "I will also send you out to preach, ¹⁵ and you will have authority to drive out demons."

¹⁶ These are the twelve he chose: Simon (Jesus gave him the name Peter); ¹⁷ James and his brother John, the sons of Zebedee (Jesus gave them the name Boanerges, which means "Men of Thunder"); ¹⁸ Andrew, Philip, Bartholomew, Matthew, Thomas, James son of Alphaeus, Thaddaeus, Simon the Patriot, ¹⁹ and Judas Iscariot, who betrayed Jesus.

Jesus and Beelzebul
(Mt 12.22–32; Lk 11.14–23; 12.10)

²⁰ Then Jesus went home. Again such a large crowd gathered that Jesus and his disciples had no time to eat. ²¹ When his family heard about it, they set out to take charge of him, because people were saying, "He's gone mad!"

²² Some teachers of the Law who had come from Jerusalem were saying, "He has Beelzebul in him! It is the chief of the demons who gives him the power to drive them out."

²³ So Jesus called them to him and spoke to them in parables: "How can Satan drive out Satan? ²⁴ If a country divides itself into groups which fight each other, that country will fall apart. ²⁵ If a family divides itself into groups which fight each other, that family will fall apart. ²⁶ So if Satan's kingdom divides into groups, it cannot last, but will fall apart and come to an end.

²⁷ "No one can break into a strong man's house and take away his belongings unless he first ties up the strong man; then he can plunder his house.

²⁸ "I assure you that people can be forgiven all their sins and all the evil things they may say. ª ²⁹ But whoever says evil things against the Holy Spirit will never be forgiven, because he has committed an eternal sin." ³⁰ (Jesus said this because some people were saying, "He has an evil spirit in him.")

Jesus' Mother and Brothers
(Mt 12.46–50; Lk 8.19–21)

³¹ Then Jesus' mother and brothers arrived. They stood outside the house and sent in a message, asking for him. ³² A crowd was sitting round Jesus, and they said to him, "Look, your mother and your brothers and sisters are outside, and they want you."

³³ Jesus answered, "Who is my mother? Who are my brothers?" ³⁴ He looked at the people sitting round him and

a **3.28** evil things they may say; *or* evil things they may say against God.

said, "Look! Here are my mother and my brothers! ³⁵ Whoever does what God wants him to do is my brother, my sister, my mother."

The Parable of the Sower
(Mt 13.1–9; Lk 8.4–8)

4 Again Jesus began to teach beside Lake Galilee. The crowd that gathered round him was so large that he got into a boat and sat in it. The boat was out in the water, and the crowd stood on the shore at the water's edge. ² He used parables to teach them many things, saying to them:

³ "Listen! Once there was a man who went out to sow corn. ⁴ As he scattered the seed in the field, some of it fell along the path, and the birds came and ate it up. ⁵ Some of it fell on rocky ground, where there was little soil. The seeds soon sprouted, because the soil wasn't deep. ⁶ Then, when the sun came up, it burnt the young plants; and because the roots had not grown deep enough, the plants soon dried up. ⁷ Some of the seed fell among thorn bushes, which grew up and choked the plants, and they didn't produce any corn. ⁸ But some seeds fell in good soil, and the plants sprouted, grew, and produced corn: some had thirty grains, others sixty, and others a hundred."

⁹ And Jesus concluded, "Listen, then, if you have ears!"

The Purpose of the Parables
(Mt 13.10–17; Lk 8.9–10)

¹⁰ When Jesus was alone, some of those who had heard him came to him with the twelve disciples and asked him to explain the parables. ¹¹ "You have been given the secret of the Kingdom of God," Jesus answered. "But the others, who are on the outside, hear all things by means of parables, ¹² so that,

'They may look and look,
    yet not see;
they may listen and listen,
    yet not understand.
For if they did, they would turn to God,
    and he would forgive them.' "

Jesus Explains the Parable of the Sower
(Mt 13.18–23; Lk 8.11–15)

¹³ Then Jesus asked them, "Don't you understand this parable? How, then, will you ever understand any parable? ¹⁴ The sower sows God's message. ¹⁵ Some people are like the seeds that fall along the path; as soon as they hear the message, Satan comes and takes it away. ¹⁶ Other people are like the seeds that fall on rocky ground. As soon as they hear the message, they receive it gladly. ¹⁷ But it does not sink deep into them, and they don't last long. So when trouble or persecution comes because of the message, they give up at once. ¹⁸ Other people are like the seeds sown among the thorn bushes. These are the ones who hear the message, ¹⁹ but the worries about this life, the love for riches, and all other kinds of desires crowd in and choke the message, and they don't bear fruit. ²⁰ But other people are like the seeds sown in good soil. They hear the message, accept it, and bear fruit: some thirty, some sixty, and some a hundred."

A Lamp under a Bowl
(Lk 8.16–18)

²¹ Jesus continued, "Does anyone ever bring in a lamp and put it under a bowl or under the bed? Doesn't he put it on the lampstand? ²² Whatever is hidden away will be brought out into the open, and whatever is covered up will be uncovered. ²³ Listen, then, if you have ears!"

²⁴ He also said to them, "Pay attention to what you hear! The same rules you use to judge others will be used by God to judge you — but with even greater severity. ²⁵ Those who have something will be given more, and those who have nothing will have taken away from them even the little they have."

The Parable of the Growing Seed

²⁶ Jesus went on to say, "The Kingdom of God is like this. A man scatters seed in his field. ²⁷ He sleeps at night, is up and about during the day, and all the while the seeds are sprouting and growing. Yet he does not know how it happens. ²⁸ The soil itself makes the plants grow and bear fruit; first the tender stalk appears, then the ear, and finally the ear full

of corn. ²⁹When the corn is ripe, the man starts cutting it with his sickle, because harvest time has come.

The Parable of the Mustard Seed
(Mt 13.31–32, 34; Lk 13.18–19)

³⁰"What shall we say the Kingdom of God is like?" asked Jesus. "What parable shall we use to explain it? ³¹It is like this. A man takes a mustard seed, the smallest seed in the world, and plants it in the ground. ³²After a while it grows up and becomes the biggest of all plants. It puts out such large branches that the birds come and make their nests in its shade."

³³Jesus preached his message to the people, using many other parables like these; he told them as much as they could understand. ³⁴He would not speak to them without using parables, but when he was alone with his disciples, he would explain everything to them.

Jesus Calms a Storm
(Mt 8.23–27; Lk 8.22–25)

³⁵On the evening of that same day Jesus said to his disciples, "Let us go across to the other side of the lake." ³⁶So they left the crowd; the disciples got into the boat in which Jesus was already sitting, and they took him with them. Other boats were there too. ³⁷Suddenly a strong wind blew

Waves began to spill over into the boat   (4.37)

up, and the waves began to spill over into the boat, so that it was about to fill with water. ³⁸ Jesus was in the back of the boat, sleeping with his head on a pillow. The disciples woke him up and said, "Teacher, don't you care that we are about to die?"

³⁹ Jesus stood up and commanded the wind, "Be quiet!" and he said to the waves, "Be still!" The wind died down, and there was a great calm. ⁴⁰ Then Jesus said to his disciples, "Why are you frightened? Have you still no faith?"

And there was a great calm   (4.39)

⁴¹ But they were terribly afraid and said to one another, "Who is this man? Even the wind and the waves obey him!"

Jesus Heals a Man with Evil Spirits
(Mt 8.28–34; Lk 8.26–39)

5 Jesus and his disciples arrived on the other side of Lake Galilee, in the territory of Gerasa. ² As soon as Jesus got out of the boat, he was met by a man who came out of the burial caves there. This man had an evil spirit in him ³ and lived among the tombs. Nobody could keep him chained up any more; ⁴ many times his feet and hands had been chained, but every time he broke the chains and smashed the irons on his feet. He was too strong for anyone to control him. ⁵ Day and night he wandered among the tombs and through the hills, screaming and cutting himself with stones.

⁶ He was some distance away when he saw Jesus; so he ran, fell on his knees before him, ⁷ and screamed in a loud voice, "Jesus, Son of the Most High God! What do you want

with me? For God's sake, I beg you, don't punish me!"
⁸(He said this because Jesus was saying, "Evil spirit, come out of this man!")

⁹So Jesus asked him, "What is your name?"

The man answered, "My name is 'Mob' — there are so many of us!" ¹⁰And he kept begging Jesus not to send the evil spirits out of that region.

¹¹There was a large herd of pigs near by, feeding on a hillside. ¹²So the spirits begged Jesus, "Send us to the pigs, and let us go into them." ¹³He let them go, and the evil spirits went out of the man and entered the pigs. The whole herd — about 2,000 pigs in all — rushed down the side of the cliff into the lake and was drowned.

¹⁴The men who had been taking care of the pigs ran away and spread the news in the town and among the farms. People went out to see what had happened, ¹⁵and when they came to Jesus, they saw the man who used to have the mob of demons in him. He was sitting there, clothed and in his right mind; and they were all afraid. ¹⁶Those who had seen it told the people what had happened to the man with the demons, and about the pigs.

¹⁷So they asked Jesus to leave their territory.

¹⁸As Jesus was getting into the boat, the man who had had the demons begged him, "Let me go with you!"

¹⁹But Jesus would not let him. Instead, he told him, "Go back home to your family and tell them how much the Lord has done for you and how kind he has been to you."

²⁰So the man left and went all through the Ten Towns, telling what Jesus had done for him. And all who heard it were amazed.

Jairus' Daughter and the Woman who Touched Jesus' Cloak
(Mt 9.18–26; Lk 8.40–56)

²¹Jesus went back across to the other side of the lake. There at the lakeside a large crowd gathered round him. ²²Jairus, an official of the local synagogue, arrived, and when he saw Jesus, he threw himself down at his feet ²³and begged him earnestly, "My little daughter is very ill. Please come and place your hands on her, so that she will get well and live!"

²⁴ Then Jesus started off with him. So many people were going along with Jesus that they were crowding him from every side.

²⁵ There was a woman who had suffered terribly from severe bleeding for twelve years, ²⁶ even though she had been treated by many doctors. She had spent all her money, but instead of getting better she got worse all the time. ²⁷ She had heard about Jesus, so she came in the crowd behind him, ²⁸ saying to herself, "If I just touch his clothes, I will get well."

²⁹ She touched his cloak, and her bleeding stopped at once; and she had the feeling inside herself that she was healed of her trouble. ³⁰ At once Jesus knew that power had gone out of him, so he turned round in the crowd and asked, "Who touched my clothes?"

³¹ His disciples answered, "You see how the people are crowding you; why do you ask who touched you?"

³² But Jesus kept looking round to see who had done it. ³³ The woman realized what had happened to her, so she came, trembling with fear, knelt at his feet, and told him the whole truth. ³⁴ Jesus said to her, "My daughter, your faith has made you well. Go in peace, and be healed of your trouble."

³⁵ While Jesus was saying this, some messengers came from Jairus' house and told him, "Your daughter has died. Why bother the Teacher any longer?"

³⁶ Jesus paid no attention to ᵃ what they said, but told him, "Don't be afraid, only believe." ³⁷ Then he did not let anyone else go on with him except Peter and James and his brother John. ³⁸ They arrived at Jairus' house, where Jesus saw the confusion and heard all the loud crying and wailing. ³⁹ He went in and said to them, "Why all this confusion? Why are you crying? The child is not dead — she is only sleeping!"

⁴⁰ They laughed at him, so he put them all out, took the child's father and mother and his three disciples, and went into the room where the child was lying. ⁴¹ He took her by the hand and said to her, "*Talitha, koum,*" which means, "Little girl, I tell you to get up!"

a **5.36** paid no attention to; *or* overheard.

⁴²She got up at once and started walking around. (She was twelve years old.) When this happened, they were completely amazed. ⁴³But Jesus gave them strict orders not to tell anyone, and he said, "Give her something to eat."

Jesus is Rejected at Nazareth
(Mt 13.53–58; Lk 4.16–30)

6 Jesus left that place and went back to his home town, followed by his disciples. ²On the Sabbath he began to teach in the synagogue. Many people were there; and when they heard him, they were all amazed. "Where did he get all this?" they asked. "What wisdom is this that has been given him? How does he perform miracles? ³Isn't he the carpenter, the son of Mary, and the brother of James, Joseph, Judas, and Simon? Aren't his sisters living here?" And so they rejected him.

⁴Jesus said to them, "Prophets are respected everywhere except in their own home town and by their relatives and their family."

⁵He was not able to perform any miracles there, except that he placed his hands on a few sick people and healed them. ⁶He was greatly surprised, because the people did not have faith.

Jesus Sends out the Twelve Disciples
(Mt 10.5–15; Lk 9.1–6)

Then Jesus went to the villages round there, teaching the people. ⁷He called the twelve disciples together and sent them out two by two. He gave them authority over the evil spirits ⁸and ordered them, "Don't take anything with you on your journey except a stick — no bread, no beggar's bag, no money in your pockets. ⁹Wear sandals, but don't carry an extra shirt." ¹⁰He also said, "Wherever you are welcomed, stay in the same house until you leave that place. ¹¹If you come to a town where people do not welcome you or will not listen to you, leave it and shake the dust off your feet. That will be a warning to them!"

¹²So they went out and preached that people should turn away from their sins. ¹³They drove out many demons, and rubbed olive oil on many sick people and healed them.

The Death of John the Baptist
(Mt 14.1–12; Lk 9.7–9)

[14] Now King Herod[a] heard about all this, because Jesus' reputation had spread everywhere. Some people were saying, "John the Baptist has come back to life! That is why he has this power to perform miracles."

[15] Others, however, said, "He is Elijah."

Others said, "He is a prophet, like one of the prophets of long ago."

[16] When Herod heard it, he said, "He is John the Baptist! I had his head cut off, but he has come back to life!" [17] Herod himself had ordered John's arrest, and he had him chained and put in prison. Herod did this because of Herodias, whom he had married, even though she was the wife of his brother Philip. [18] John the Baptist kept telling Herod, "It isn't right for you to be married to your brother's wife!"

[19] So Herodias held a grudge against John and wanted to kill him, but she could not because of Herod. [20] Herod was afraid of John because he knew that John was a good and holy man, and so he kept him safe. He liked to listen to him, even though he became greatly disturbed every time he heard him.

[21] Finally Herodias got her chance. It was on Herod's birthday, when he gave a feast for all the chief government officials, the military commanders, and the leading citizens of Galilee. [22] The daughter of Herodias[b] came in and danced, and pleased Herod and his guests. So the king said to the girl, "What would you like to have? I will give you anything you want." [23] With many vows he said to her, "I swear that I will give you anything you ask for, even as much as half my kingdom!"

[24] So the girl went out and asked her mother, "What shall I ask for?"

"The head of John the Baptist," she answered.

a **6.14** KING HEROD: *Herod Antipas, ruler of Galilee.*
b **6.22** The daughter of Herodias; *some manuscripts have* His daughter Herodias.

²⁵ The girl hurried back at once to the king and demanded, "I want you to give me here and now the head of John the Baptist on a dish!"

²⁶ This made the king very sad, but he could not refuse her because of the vows he had made in front of all his guests. ²⁷ So he sent off a guard at once with orders to bring John's head. The guard left, went to the prison, and cut John's head off; ²⁸ then he brought it on a dish and gave it to the girl, who gave it to her mother. ²⁹ When John's disciples heard about this, they came and took away his body, and buried it.

Jesus Feeds a Great Crowd
(Mt 14.13–21; Lk 9.10–17; Jn 6.1–14)

³⁰ The apostles returned and met with Jesus, and told him all they had done and taught. ³¹ There were so many people coming and going that Jesus and his disciples didn't even have time to eat. So he said to them, "Let us go off by ourselves to some place where we will be alone and you can rest for a while." ³² So they started out in a boat by themselves for a lonely place.

³³ Many people, however, saw them leave and knew at once who they were; so they went from all the towns and ran ahead by land and arrived at the place ahead of Jesus and his disciples. ³⁴ When Jesus got out of the boat, he saw this large crowd, and his heart was filled with pity for them, because they were like sheep without a shepherd. So he began to teach them many things. ³⁵ When it was getting late, his disciples came to him and said, "It is already very late, and this is a lonely place. ³⁶ Send the people away, and let them go to the nearby farms and villages in order to buy themselves something to eat."

³⁷ "You yourselves give them something to eat," Jesus answered.

They asked, "Do you want us to go and spend two hundred silver coins[a] on bread in order to feed them?"

³⁸ So Jesus asked them, "How much bread have you got? Go and see."

a **6.37** SILVER COINS: *A silver coin was the daily wage of a rural worker (see Mt 20.2).*

When they found out, they told him, "Five loaves and also two fish."

³⁹ Jesus then told his disciples to make all the people divide into groups and sit down on the green grass. ⁴⁰ So the people sat down in rows, in groups of a hundred and groups of fifty. ⁴¹ Then Jesus took the five loaves and the two fish, looked up to heaven, and gave thanks to God. He broke the loaves and gave them to his disciples to distribute to the people. He also divided the two fish among them all. ⁴² Everyone ate and had enough. ⁴³ Then the disciples took up twelve baskets full of what was left of the bread and the fish. ⁴⁴ The number of men who were fed was 5,000.

Jesus Walks on the Water
(Mt 14.22–33; Jn 6.15–21)

⁴⁵ At once Jesus made his disciples get into the boat and go ahead of him to Bethsaida, on the other side of the lake, while he sent the crowd away. ⁴⁶ After saying goodbye to the people he went away to a hill to pray. ⁴⁷ When evening came, the boat was in the middle of the lake, while Jesus was alone on land. ⁴⁸ He saw that his disciples were straining at the oars, because they were rowing against the wind; so some time between three and six o'clock in the morning he came to them, walking on the water. He was going to pass them by, ᵃ ⁴⁹ but they saw him walking on the water. "It's a ghost!" they thought, and screamed. ⁵⁰ They were all terrified when they saw him.

It's a ghost!   (6.49)

a **6.48** pass them by; *or* join them.

Jesus spoke to them at once, "Courage!" he said. "It is I. Don't be afraid!" [51] Then he got into the boat with them, and the wind died down. The disciples were completely amazed, [52] because they had not understood the real meaning of the feeding of the 5,000; their minds could not grasp it.

Jesus Heals the Sick in Gennesaret
(Mt 14.34–36)

[53] They crossed the lake and came to land at Gennesaret, where they tied up the boat. [54] As they left the boat, people recognized Jesus at once. [55] So they ran throughout the whole region; and wherever they heard he was, they brought to him sick people lying on their mats. [56] And everywhere Jesus went, to villages, towns, or farms, people would take those who were ill to the market places and beg him to let them at least touch the edge of his cloak; and all who touched it were made well.

The Teaching of the Ancestors
(Mt 15.1–9)

7 Some Pharisees and teachers of the Law who had come from Jerusalem gathered round Jesus. [2] They noticed that some of his disciples were eating their food with hands that were ritually unclean — that is, they had not washed them in the way the Pharisees said people should.

[3] (For the Pharisees, as well as the rest of the Jews, follow the teaching they received from their ancestors: they do not eat unless they wash their hands in the proper way; [4] nor do they eat anything that comes from the market unless they wash it first. [a] And they follow many other rules which they have received, such as the proper way to wash cups, pots, copper bowls, and beds. [b])

[5] So the Pharisees and the teachers of the Law asked Jesus, "Why is it that your disciples do not follow the teaching handed down by our ancestors, but instead eat with ritually unclean hands?"

a **7.4** anything that comes from the market unless they wash it first; *or* anything after they come from the market unless they wash themselves first.

b **7.4** *Some manuscripts do not have* and beds.

⁶Jesus answered them, "How right Isaiah was when he prophesied about you! You are hypocrites, just as he wrote:

'These people, says God, honour me with their words,
    but their heart is really far away from me.
⁷It is no use for them to worship me,
    because they teach human rules
    as though they were God's laws!'

⁸"You put aside God's command and obey human teachings."

⁹And Jesus continued, "You have a clever way of rejecting God's law in order to uphold your own teaching. ¹⁰For Moses commanded, 'Respect your father and your mother,' and, 'Whoever curses his father or his mother is to be put to death.' ¹¹But you teach that if a person has something he could use to help his father or mother, but says, 'This is Corban' (which means, it belongs to God), ¹²he is excused from helping his father or mother. ¹³In this way the teaching you pass on to others cancels out the word of God. And there are many other things like this that you do."

The Things that Make a Person Unclean
(Mt 15.10–20)

¹⁴Then Jesus called the crowd to him once more and said to them, "Listen to me, all of you, and understand. ¹⁵There is nothing that goes into a person from the outside which can make him ritually unclean. Rather, it is what comes out of a person that makes him unclean." [a]

¹⁷When he left the crowd and went into the house, his disciples asked him to explain this saying. ¹⁸"You are no more intelligent than the others," Jesus said to them. "Don't you understand? Nothing that goes into a person from the outside can really make him unclean, ¹⁹because it does not go into his heart but into his stomach and then goes on out of the body." (In saying this, Jesus declared that all foods are fit to be eaten.)

²⁰And he went on to say, "It is what comes out of a person that makes him unclean. ²¹For from the inside,

a **7.15** *Some manuscripts add verse 16:* Listen, then, if you have ears! *(see 4.23).*

from a person's heart, come the evil ideas which lead him
to do immoral things, to rob, kill, ²²commit adultery, be
greedy, and do all sorts of evil things; deceit, indecency,
jealousy, slander, pride, and folly — ²³all these evil things
come from inside a person and make him unclean."

A Woman's Faith
(Mt 15.21–28)

²⁴Then Jesus left and went away to the territory near
the city of Tyre. He went into a house and did not want
anyone to know he was there, but he could not stay hidden.
²⁵A woman, whose daughter had an evil spirit in her, heard
about Jesus and came to him at once and fell at his feet.
²⁶The woman was a Gentile, born in the region of
Phoenicia in Syria. She begged Jesus to drive the demon
out of her daughter. ²⁷But Jesus answered, "Let us first
feed the children. It isn't right to take the children's food
and throw it to the dogs."

²⁸"Sir," she answered, "even the dogs under the table
eat the children's leftovers!"

²⁹So Jesus said to her, "Because of that answer, go back
home, where you will find that the demon has gone out of
your daughter!"

³⁰She went home and found her child lying on the bed;
the demon had indeed gone out of her.

Jesus Heals a Deaf-mute

³¹Jesus then left the neighbourhood of Tyre and went
on through Sidon to Lake Galilee, going by way of the
territory of the Ten Towns. ³²Some people brought him a
man who was deaf and could hardly speak, and they
begged Jesus to place his hands on him. ³³So Jesus took
him off alone, away from the crowd, put his fingers in the
man's ears, spat, and touched the man's tongue. ³⁴Then
Jesus looked up to heaven, gave a deep groan, and said to
the man, "*Ephphatha*," which means, "Open up!"

³⁵At once the man was able to hear, his speech impedi-
ment was removed, and he began to talk without any
trouble. ³⁶Then Jesus ordered the people not to speak of
it to anyone; but the more he ordered them not to, the more

they spoke. ³⁷ And all who heard were completely amazed. "How well he does everything!" they exclaimed. "He even causes the deaf to hear and the dumb to speak!"

Jesus Feeds Four Thousand People
(Mt 15.32–39)

8 Not long afterwards another large crowd came together. When the people had nothing left to eat, Jesus called the disciples to him and said, ² "I feel sorry for these people, because they have been with me for three days and now have nothing to eat. ³ If I send them home without feeding them, they will faint as they go, because some of them have come a long way."

⁴ His disciples asked him, "Where in this desert can anyone find enough food to feed all these people?"

⁵ "How much bread have you got?" Jesus asked.

"Seven loaves," they answered.

⁶ He ordered the crowd to sit down on the ground. Then he took the seven loaves, gave thanks to God, broke them, and gave them to his disciples to distribute to the crowd; and the disciples did so. ⁷ They also had a few small fish. Jesus gave thanks for these and told the disciples to distribute them too. ⁸⁻⁹ Everybody ate and had enough — there were about 4,000 people. Then the disciples took up seven baskets full of pieces left over. Jesus sent the people away ¹⁰ and at once got into a boat with his disciples and went to the district of Dalmanutha.

The Pharisees Ask for a Miracle
(Mt 12.38–42; 16.1–4)

¹¹ Some Pharisees came to Jesus and started to argue with him. They wanted to trap him, so they asked him to perform a miracle to show that God approved of him. ¹² But Jesus gave a deep groan and said, "Why do the people of this day ask for a miracle? No, I tell you! No such proof will be given to these people!"

¹³ He left them, got back into the boat, and started across to the other side of the lake.

The Yeast of the Pharisees and of Herod
(Mt 16.5–12)

¹⁴ The disciples had forgotten to bring enough bread and had only one loaf with them in the boat. ¹⁵ "Take care," Jesus warned them, "and be on your guard against the yeast of the Pharisees and the yeast of Herod."

¹⁶ They started discussing among themselves: "He says this because we haven't any bread."

¹⁷ Jesus knew what they were saying, so he asked them, "Why are you discussing about not having any bread? Don't you know or understand yet? Are your minds so dull? ¹⁸ You have eyes — can't you see? You have ears — can't you hear? Don't you remember ¹⁹ when I broke the five loaves for the five thousand people? How many baskets full of leftover pieces did you take up?"

"Twelve," they answered.

²⁰ "And when I broke the seven loaves for the four thousand people," asked Jesus, "how many baskets full of leftover pieces did you take up?"

"Seven," they answered.

²¹ "And you still don't understand?" he asked them.

Jesus Heals a Blind Man at Bethsaida

²² They came to Bethsaida, where some people brought a blind man to Jesus and begged him to touch him. ²³ Jesus took the blind man by the hand and led him out of the village. After spitting on the man's eyes, Jesus placed his hands on him and asked him, "Can you see anything?"

²⁴ The man looked up and said, "Yes, I can see people, but they look like trees walking about."

²⁵ Jesus again placed his hands on the man's eyes. This time the man looked intently, his eyesight returned, and he saw everything clearly. ²⁶ Jesus then sent him home with the order, "Don't go back into the village."

Peter's Declaration about Jesus
(Mt 16.13–20; Lk 9.18–21)

²⁷ Then Jesus and his disciples went away to the villages near Caesarea Philippi. On the way he asked them, "Tell me, who do people say I am?"

²⁸ "Some say that you are John the Baptist," they answered; "others say that you are Elijah, while others say that you are one of the prophets."

²⁹ "What about you?" he asked them. "Who do you say I am?"

Peter answered, "You are the Messiah."

³⁰ Then Jesus ordered them, "Do not tell anyone about me."

Jesus Speaks about his Suffering and Death
(Mt 16.21–28; Lk 9.22–27)

³¹ Then Jesus began to teach his disciples: "The Son of Man must suffer much and be rejected by the elders, the chief priests, and the teachers of the Law. He will be put to death, but three days later he will rise to life." ³² He made this very clear to them. So Peter took him aside and began to rebuke him. ³³ But Jesus turned round, looked at his disciples, and rebuked Peter. "Get away from me, Satan," he said. "Your thoughts don't come from God but from human nature!"

³⁴ Then Jesus called the crowd and his disciples to him. "If anyone wants to come with me," he told them, "he must forget self, carry his cross, and follow me. ³⁵ For whoever wants to save his own life will lose it; but whoever loses his life for me and for the gospel will save it. ³⁶ Do people gain anything if they win the whole world but lose their life? Of

He must forget self, carry his cross, and follow me   (8.34)

course not! [37] There is nothing they can give to regain their life. [38] If a person is ashamed of me and of my teaching in this godless and wicked day, then the Son of Man will be ashamed of him when he comes in the glory of his Father with the holy angels."

9 And he went on to say, "I tell you, there are some here who will not die until they have seen the Kingdom of God come with power."

The Transfiguration
(Mt 17.1–13; Lk 9.28–36)

[2] Six days later Jesus took with him Peter, James, and John, and led them up a high mountain, where they were alone. As they looked on, a change came over Jesus, [3] and his clothes became shining white — whiter than anyone in the world could wash them. [4] Then the three disciples saw Elijah and Moses talking with Jesus. [5] Peter spoke up and said to Jesus, "Teacher, how good it is that we are here! We will make three tents, one for you, one for Moses, and one for Elijah." [6] He and the others were so frightened that he did not know what to say.

[7] Then a cloud appeared and covered them with its shadow, and a voice came from the cloud, "This is my own dear Son — listen to him!" [8] They took a quick look round but did not see anyone else; only Jesus was with them.

[9] As they came down the mountain, Jesus ordered them, "Don't tell anyone what you have seen, until the Son of Man has risen from death."

[10] They obeyed his order, but among themselves they started discussing the matter, "What does this 'rising from death' mean?" [11] And they asked Jesus, "Why do the teachers of the Law say that Elijah has to come first?"

[12] His answer was, "Elijah is indeed coming first in order to get everything ready. Yet why do the Scriptures say that the Son of Man will suffer much and be rejected? [13] I tell you, however, that Elijah has already come and that people treated him just as they pleased, as the Scriptures say about him."

Jesus Heals a Boy with an Evil Spirit
(Mt 17.14–21; Lk 9.37–43a)

¹⁴When they joined the rest of the disciples, they saw a large crowd round them and some teachers of the Law arguing with them. ¹⁵When the people saw Jesus, they were greatly surprised, and ran to him and greeted him. ¹⁶Jesus asked his disciples, "What are you arguing with them about?"

¹⁷A man in the crowd answered, "Teacher, I brought my son to you, because he has an evil spirit in him and cannot talk. ¹⁸Whenever the spirit attacks him, it throws him to the ground, and he foams at the mouth, grits his teeth, and becomes stiff all over. I asked your disciples to drive the spirit out, but they could not."

¹⁹Jesus said to them, "How unbelieving you people are! How long must I stay with you? How long do I have to put up with you? Bring the boy to me!" ²⁰They brought him to Jesus.

As soon as the spirit saw Jesus, it threw the boy into a fit, so that he fell on the ground and rolled round, foaming at the mouth. ²¹"How long has he been like this?" Jesus asked the father.

"Ever since he was a child," he replied. ²²"Many times the evil spirit has tried to kill him by throwing him in the fire and into water. Have pity on us and help us, if you possibly can!"

²³"Yes," said Jesus, "if you yourself can! Everything is possible for the person who has faith."

²⁴The father at once cried out, "I do have faith, but not enough. Help me to have more!"

²⁵Jesus noticed that the crowd was closing in on them, so he gave a command to the evil spirit. "Deaf and dumb spirit," he said, "I order you to come out of the boy and never go into him again!"

²⁶The spirit screamed, threw the boy into a bad fit, and came out. The boy looked like a corpse, and everyone said, "He is dead!" ²⁷But Jesus took the boy by the hand and helped him to rise, and he stood up.

²⁸After Jesus had gone indoors, his disciples asked him privately, "Why couldn't we drive the spirit out?"

²⁹ "Only prayer can drive this kind out," answered Jesus; "nothing else can."

Jesus Speaks Again about his Death
(Mt 17.22–23; Lk 9.43b–45)

³⁰ Jesus and his disciples left that place and went on through Galilee. Jesus did not want anyone to know where he was, ³¹ because he was teaching his disciples: "The Son of Man will be handed over to those who will kill him. Three days later, however, he will rise to life."

³² But they did not understand what this teaching meant, and they were afraid to ask him.

Who is the Greatest?
(Mt 18.1–5; Lk 9.46–48)

³³ They came to Capernaum, and after going indoors Jesus asked his disciples, "What were you arguing about on the road?"

³⁴ But they would not answer him, because on the road they had been arguing among themselves about who was the greatest. ³⁵ Jesus sat down, called the twelve disciples, and said to them, "Whoever wants to be first must place himself last of all and be the servant of all." ³⁶ Then he took a child and made him stand in front of them. He put his arms round him and said to them, ³⁷ "Whoever welcomes in my name one of these children, welcomes me; and whoever welcomes me, welcomes not only me but also the one who sent me."

Whoever is not Against Us is For Us
(Lk 9.49–50)

³⁸ John said to him, "Teacher, we saw a man who was driving out demons in your name, and we told him to stop, because he doesn't belong to our group."

³⁹ "Do not try to stop him," Jesus told them, "because no one who performs a miracle in my name will be able soon afterwards to say evil things about me. ⁴⁰ For whoever is not against us is for us. ⁴¹ I assure you that anyone who gives you a drink of water because you belong to me will certainly receive his reward.

Temptations to Sin
(Mt 18.6–9; Lk 17.1–2)

⁴²"If anyone should cause one of these little ones to lose his faith in me, it would be better for that person to have a large millstone tied round his neck and be thrown into the sea. ⁴³So if your hand makes you lose your faith, cut it off! It is better for you to enter life without a hand than to keep both hands and go off to hell, to the fire that never goes out. ᵃ ⁴⁵And if your foot makes you lose your faith, cut it off! It is better for you to enter life without a foot than to keep both feet and be thrown into hell. ᵇ ⁴⁷And if your eye makes you lose your faith, take it out! It is better for you to enter the Kingdom of God with only one eye than to keep both eyes and be thrown into hell. ⁴⁸There 'the worms that eat them never die, and the fire that burns them is never put out.'

⁴⁹"Everyone will be purified by fire as a sacrifice is purified by salt.

⁵⁰"Salt is good; but if it loses its saltiness, how can you make it salty again?

"Have the salt of friendship among yourselves, and live in peace with one another."

Jesus Teaches about Divorce
(Mt 19.1–12; Lk 16.18)

10 Then Jesus left that place, went to the province of Judea, and crossed the River Jordan. Crowds came flocking to him again, and he taught them, as he always did.

²Some Pharisees came to him and tried to trap him. "Tell us," they asked, "does our Law allow a man to divorce his wife?"

³Jesus answered with a question, "What law did Moses give you?"

⁴Their answer was, "Moses gave permission for a man to write a divorce notice and send his wife away."

a **9.43** *Some manuscripts add verse 44:* There 'the worms that eat them never die, and the fire that burns them is never put out' *(see verse 48).*

b **9.45** *Some manuscripts add verse 46:* There 'the worms that eat them never die, and the fire that burns them is never put out'*(see verse 48).*

⁵ Jesus said to them, "Moses wrote this law for you because you are so hard to teach. ⁶ But in the beginning, at the time of creation, 'God made them male and female,' as the scripture says. ⁷ 'And for this reason a man will leave his father and mother and unite with his wife,ᵃ ⁸ and the two will become one.' So they are no longer two, but one. ⁹ No human being then must separate what God has joined together."

¹⁰ When they went back into the house, the disciples asked Jesus about this matter. ¹¹ He said to them, "A man who divorces his wife and marries another woman commits adultery against his wife. ¹² In the same way, a woman who divorces her husband and marries another man commits adultery."

Jesus Blesses Little Children
(Mt 19.13–15; Lk 18.15–17)

¹³ Some people brought children to Jesus for him to place his hands on them, but the disciples scolded the people. ¹⁴ When Jesus noticed this, he was angry and said to his disciples, "Let the children come to me, and do not stop them, because the Kingdom of God belongs to such as these. ¹⁵ I assure you that whoever does not receive the Kingdom of God like a child will never enter it." ¹⁶ Then he took the children in his arms, placed his hands on each of them, and blessed them.

The Rich Man
(Mt 19.16–30; Lk 18.18–30)

¹⁷ As Jesus was starting on his way again, a man ran up, knelt before him, and asked him, "Good Teacher, what must I do to receive eternal life?"

¹⁸ "Why do you call me good?" Jesus asked him. "No one is good except God alone. ¹⁹ You know the commandments: 'Do not commit murder; do not commit adultery; do not steal; do not accuse anyone falsely; do not cheat; respect your father and your mother.' "

²⁰ "Teacher," the man said, "ever since I was young, I have obeyed all these commandments."

a **10.7** *Some manuscripts do not have* and unite with his wife.

²¹ Jesus looked straight at him with love and said, "You need only one thing. Go and sell all you have and give the money to the poor, and you will have riches in heaven; then come and follow me." ²² When the man heard this, gloom spread over his face, and he went away sad, because he was very rich.

²³ Jesus looked round at his disciples and said to them, "How hard it will be for rich people to enter the Kingdom of God!"

²⁴ The disciples were shocked at these words, but Jesus went on to say, "My children, how hard it is to enter the Kingdom of God! ²⁵ It is much harder for a rich person to enter the Kingdom of God than for a camel to go through the eye of a needle."

²⁶ At this the disciples were completely amazed and asked one another, "Who, then, can be saved?"

²⁷ Jesus looked straight at them and answered, "This is impossible for human beings, but not for God; everything is possible for God."

²⁸ Then Peter spoke up, "Look, we have left everything and followed you."

²⁹ "Yes," Jesus said to them, "and I tell you that anyone who leaves home or brothers or sisters or mother or father or children or fields for me and for the gospel, ³⁰ will receive much more in this present age. He will receive a hundred times more houses, brothers, sisters, mothers, children and fields — and persecutions as well; and in the age to come he will receive eternal life. ³¹ But many who now are first will be last, and many who now are last will be first."

Jesus Speaks a Third Time about his Death
(Mt 20.17–19; Lk 18.31–34)

³² Jesus and his disciples were now on the road going up to Jerusalem. Jesus was going ahead of the disciples, who were filled with alarm; the people who followed behind were afraid. Once again Jesus took the twelve disciples aside and spoke of the things that were going to happen to him. ³³ "Listen," he told them, "we are going up to Jerusalem where the Son of Man will be handed over to the chief priests and the teachers of the Law. They will

condemn him to death and then hand him over to the
Gentiles, ³⁴ who will mock him, spit on him, whip him, and
kill him; but three days later he will rise to life."

The Request of James and John
(Mt 20.20–28)

³⁵ Then James and John, the sons of Zebedee, came to
Jesus. "Teacher," they said, "there is something we want you
to do for us."

³⁶ "What is it?" Jesus asked them.

³⁷ They answered, "When you sit on your throne in your
glorious Kingdom, we want you to let us sit with you, one
at your right and one at your left."

³⁸ Jesus said to them, "You don't know what you are
asking for. Can you drink the cup of suffering that I must
drink? Can you be baptized in the way I must be baptized?"

³⁹ "We can," they answered.

Jesus said to them, "You will indeed drink the cup I must
drink and be baptized in the way I must be baptized. ⁴⁰ But
I do not have the right to choose who will sit at my right and
my left. It is God who will give these places to those for whom
he has prepared them."

⁴¹ When the other ten disciples heard about it, they
became angry with James and John. ⁴² So Jesus called them
all together to him and said, "You know that those who are
considered rulers of the heathen have power over them, and
the leaders have complete authority. ⁴³ This, however, is
not the way it is among you. If one of you wants to be great,
he must be the servant of the rest; ⁴⁴ and if one of you wants
to be first, he must be the slave of all. ⁴⁵ For even the Son of
Man did not come to be served; he came to serve and to give
his life to redeem many people."

Jesus Heals Blind Bartimaeus
(Mt 20.29–34; Lk 18.35–43)

⁴⁶ They came to Jericho, and as Jesus was leaving with his
disciples and a large crowd, a blind beggar named Bar-
timaeus son of Timaeus was sitting by the road. ⁴⁷ When he
heard that it was Jesus of Nazareth, he began to shout,
"Jesus! Son of David! Take pity on me!"

⁴⁸ Many of the people scolded him and told him to be quiet. But he shouted even more loudly, "Son of David, take pity on me!"

⁴⁹ Jesus stopped and said, "Call him."

So they called the blind man. "Cheer up!" they said. "Get up, he is calling you."

⁵⁰ He threw off his cloak, jumped up, and came to Jesus.

⁵¹ "What do you want me to do for you?" Jesus asked him.

"Teacher," the blind man answered, "I want to see again."

⁵² "Go," Jesus told him, "your faith has made you well."

At once he was able to see and followed Jesus on the road.

The Triumphant Entry into Jerusalem
(Mt 21.1–11; Lk 19.28–40; Jn 12.12–19)

11 As they approached Jerusalem, near the towns of Bethphage and Bethany, they came to the Mount of Olives. Jesus sent two of his disciples on ahead ² with these instructions: "Go to the village there ahead of you. As soon as you get there, you will find a colt tied up that has never been ridden. Untie it and bring it here. ³ And if someone asks you why you are doing that, tell him that the Master ᵃ needs it and will send it back at once."

⁴ So they went and found a colt out in the street, tied to the door of a house. As they were untying it, ⁵ some of the bystanders asked them, "What are you doing, untying that colt?"

⁶ They answered just as Jesus had told them, and the bystanders let them go. ⁷ They brought the colt to Jesus, threw their cloaks over the animal, and Jesus got on. ⁸ Many people spread their cloaks on the road, while others cut branches in the fields and spread them on the road. ⁹ The people who were in front and those who followed behind began to shout, "Praise God! God bless him who comes in the name of the Lord! ¹⁰ God bless the coming kingdom of King David, our father! Praise God!"

a **11.3** the Master; *or* its owner.

¹¹ Jesus entered Jerusalem, went into the Temple, and looked round at everything. But since it was already late in the day, he went out to Bethany with the twelve disciples.

Jesus Curses the Fig Tree
(Mt 21.18–19)

¹² The next day, as they were coming back from Bethany, Jesus was hungry. ¹³ He saw in the distance a fig tree covered with leaves, so he went to see if he could find any figs on it. But when he came to it, he found only leaves, because it was not the right time for figs. ¹⁴ Jesus said to the fig tree, "No one shall ever eat figs from you again!"

And his disciples heard him.

Jesus Goes to the Temple
(Mt 21.12–17; Lk 19.45–48; Jn 2.13–22)

¹⁵ When they arrived in Jerusalem, Jesus went to the Temple and began to drive out all those who were buying and selling. He overturned the tables of the money-changers and the stools of those who sold pigeons, ¹⁶ and he would not let anyone carry anything through the temple courtyards. ¹⁷ He then taught the people: "It is written in the Scriptures that God said, 'My Temple will be called a house of prayer for the people of all nations.' But you have turned it into a hideout for thieves!"

¹⁸ The chief priests and the teachers of the Law heard of this, so they began looking for some way to kill Jesus. They were afraid of him, because the whole crowd was amazed at his teaching.

¹⁹ When evening came, Jesus and his disciples left the city.

The Lesson from the Fig Tree
(Mt 21.20–22)

²⁰ Early next morning, as they walked along the road, they saw the fig tree. It was dead all the way down to its roots. ²¹ Peter remembered what had happened and said to Jesus, "Look, Teacher, the fig tree you cursed has died!"

²² Jesus answered them, "Have faith in God. ²³ I assure you that whoever tells this hill to get up and throw itself in the sea and does not doubt in his heart, but believes that what he says will happen, it will be done for him. ²⁴ For this reason I tell you: when you pray and ask for something, believe that you have received it, and you will be given whatever you ask for. ²⁵ And when you stand and pray, forgive anything you may have against anyone, so that your Father in heaven will forgive the wrongs you have done." ᵃ

The Question about Jesus' Authority
(Mt 21.23–27; Lk 20.1–8)

²⁷ They arrived once again in Jerusalem. As Jesus was walking in the Temple, the chief priests, the teachers of the Law, and the elders came to him ²⁸ and asked him, "What right have you to do these things? Who gave you this right?"

²⁹ Jesus answered them, "I will ask you just one question, and if you give me an answer, I will tell you what right I have to do these things. ³⁰ Tell me, where did John's right to baptize come from: was it from God or from human beings?"

³¹ They started to argue among themselves: "What shall we say? If we answer, 'From God,' he will say, 'Why, then, did you not believe John?' ³² But if we say, 'From human beings . . .' " (They were afraid of the people, because everyone was convinced that John had been a prophet.) ³³ So their answer to Jesus was, "We don't know."

Jesus said to them, "Neither will I tell you, then, by what right I do these things."

The Parable of the Tenants in the Vineyard
(Mt 21.33–46; Lk 20.9–19)

12 Then Jesus spoke to them in parables: "Once there was a man who planted a vineyard, put a fence round it, dug a hole for the winepress, and built a watchtower.

a **11.25** *Some manuscripts add verse 26:* If you do not forgive others, your Father in heaven will not forgive the wrongs you have done *(see Mt 6.15).*

Then he let out the vineyard to tenants and left home on a journey. ² When the time came to gather the grapes, he sent a slave to the tenants to receive from them his share of the harvest. ³ The tenants seized the slave, beat him, and sent him back without a thing. ⁴ Then the owner sent another slave; the tenants beat him over the head and treated him shamefully. ⁵ The owner sent another slave, and they killed him; and they treated many others the same way, beating some and killing others. ⁶ The only one left to send was the man's own dear son. Last of all, then, he sent his son to the tenants. 'I am sure they will respect my son,' he said. ⁷ But those tenants said to one another, 'This is the owner's son. Come on, let's kill him, and his property will be ours!' ⁸ So they seized the son and killed him and threw his body out of the vineyard.

⁹ "What, then, will the owner of the vineyard do?" asked Jesus. "He will come and kill those tenants and hand the vineyard over to others. ¹⁰ Surely you have read this scripture:

'The stone which the builders rejected as worthless
    turned out to be the most important of all.
¹¹ This was done by the Lord;
    what a wonderful sight it is!' "

¹² The Jewish leaders tried to arrest Jesus, because they knew that he had told this parable against them. But they were afraid of the crowd, so they left him and went away.

The Question about Paying Taxes
(Mt 22.15–22; Lk 20.20–26)

¹³ Some Pharisees and some members of Herod's party were sent to Jesus to trap him with questions. ¹⁴ They came to him and said, "Teacher, we know that you tell the truth, without worrying about what people think. You pay no attention to anyone's status, but teach the truth about God's will for people. Tell us, is it against our Law to pay taxes to the Roman Emperor? Should we pay them or not?"

¹⁵ But Jesus saw through their trick and answered, "Why are you trying to trap me? Bring a silver coin, and let me see it."

¹⁶They brought him one, and he asked, "Whose face and name are these?"

"The Emperor's," they answered.

¹⁷So Jesus said, "Well, then, pay the Emperor what belongs to the Emperor, and pay God what belongs to God."

And they were amazed at Jesus.

The Question about Rising from Death
(Mt 22.23–33; Lk 20.27–40)

¹⁸Then some Sadducees, who say that people will not rise from death, came to Jesus and said, ¹⁹"Teacher, Moses wrote this law for us: 'If a man dies and leaves a wife but no children, that man's brother must marry the widow so that they can have children who will be considered the dead man's children.' ²⁰Once there were seven brothers; the eldest got married and died without having children. ²¹Then the second one married the woman, and he also died without having children. The same thing happened to the third brother, ²²and then to the rest: all seven brothers married the woman and died without having children. Last of all, the woman died. ²³Now, when all the dead rise to life on the day of resurrection, whose wife will she be? All seven of them had married her."

²⁴Jesus answered them, "How wrong you are! And do you know why? It is because you don't know the Scriptures or God's power. ²⁵For when the dead rise to life, they will be like the angels in heaven and will not marry. ²⁶Now, as for the dead being raised: haven't you ever read in the Book of Moses the passage about the burning bush? There it is written that God said to Moses, 'I am the God of Abraham, the God of Isaac, and the God of Jacob.' ²⁷He is the God of the living, not of the dead. You are completely wrong!"

The Great Commandment
(Mt 22.34–40; Lk 10.25–28)

²⁸A teacher of the Law was there who heard the discussion. He saw that Jesus had given the Sadducees a good answer, so he came to him with a question: "Which commandment is the most important of all?"

²⁹ Jesus replied, "The most important one is this: 'Listen, Israel! The Lord our God is the only Lord. ᵃ ³⁰ Love the Lord your God with all your heart, with all your soul, with all your mind, and with all your strength.' ³¹ The second most important commandment is this: 'Love your neighbour as you love yourself.' There is no other commandment more important than these two."

³² The teacher of the Law said to Jesus, "Well done, Teacher! It is true, as you say, that only the Lord is God and that there is no other god but he. ³³ And to love God with all your heart and with all your mind and with all your strength, and to love your neighbour as yourself, is more important than to offer animals and other sacrifices to God."

³⁴ Jesus noticed how wise his answer was, and so he told him, "You are not far from the Kingdom of God."

After this nobody dared to ask Jesus any more questions.

The Question about the Messiah
(Mt 22.41–46; Lk 20.41–44)

³⁵ As Jesus was teaching in the Temple, he asked the question, "How can the teachers of the Law say that the Messiah will be the descendant of David? ³⁶ The Holy Spirit inspired David to say:

'The Lord said to my Lord:
    Sit here on my right
    until I put your enemies under your feet.'

³⁷ David himself called him 'Lord'; so how can the Messiah be David's descendant?"

Jesus Warns against the Teachers of the Law
(Mt 23.1–36; Lk 20.45–47)

A large crowd was listening to Jesus gladly. ³⁸ As he taught them, he said, "Watch out for the teachers of the Law, who like to walk around in their long robes and be greeted with respect in the market place, ³⁹ who choose the reserved seats in the synagogues and the best places at feasts. ⁴⁰ They take advantage of widows and rob them

a **12.29** The Lord our God is the only Lord; or The Lord is our God, the Lord alone.

A poor widow came along   (12.42)

of their homes, and then make a show of saying long
prayers. Their punishment will be all the worse!"

The Widow's Offering
(Lk 21.1–4)

⁴¹ As Jesus sat near the temple treasury, he watched
the people as they dropped in their money. Many rich
men dropped in a lot of money; ⁴² then a poor widow
came along and dropped in two little copper coins, worth
about a penny. ⁴³ He called his disciples together and said to
them, "I tell you that this poor widow put more in the
offering box than all the others. ⁴⁴ For the others put in what
they had to spare of their riches; but she, poor as she is, put
in all she had — she gave all she had to live on."

Jesus Speaks of the Destruction of the Temple
(Mt 24.1–2; Lk 21.5–6)

13 As Jesus was leaving the Temple, one of his disciples
said, "Look, Teacher! What wonderful stones and
buildings!"

² Jesus answered, "You see these great buildings? Not a single stone here will be left in its place; every one of them will be thrown down."

Troubles and Persecutions
(Mt 24.3–14; Lk 21.7–19)

³ Jesus was sitting on the Mount of Olives, across from the Temple, when Peter, James, John, and Andrew came to him in private. ⁴ "Tell us when this will be," they said, "and tell us what will happen to show that the time has come for all these things to take place."

⁵ Jesus said to them, "Be on guard, and don't let anyone deceive you. ⁶ Many men, claiming to speak for me, will come and say, 'I am he!' and they will deceive many people. ⁷ And don't be troubled when you hear the noise of battles close by and news of battles far away. Such things must happen, but they do not mean that the end has come. ⁸ Countries will fight each other; kingdoms will attack one another. There will be earthquakes everywhere, and there will be famines. These things are like the first pains of childbirth.

⁹ "You yourselves must be on guard. You will be arrested and taken to court. You will be beaten in the synagogues; you will stand before rulers and kings for my sake to tell them the Good News. ¹⁰ But before the end comes, the gospel must be preached to all peoples. ¹¹ And when you are arrested and taken to court, do not worry beforehand about what you are going to say; when the time comes, say whatever is then given to you. For the words you speak will not be yours; they will come from the Holy Spirit. ¹² Men will hand over their own brothers to be put to death, and fathers will do the same to their children. Children will turn against their parents and have them put to death. ¹³ Everyone will hate you because of me. But whoever holds out to the end will be saved.

The Awful Horror
(Mt 24.15–28; Lk 21.20–24)

¹⁴ "You will see 'The Awful Horror' standing in the place where he should not be." (Note to the reader: be sure to understand what this means!) "Then those who are in Judea must run away to the hills. ¹⁵ Someone who is on the roof of

his house must not lose time by going down into the house to get anything to take with him. [16] Someone who is in the field must not go back to the house for his cloak. [17] How terrible it will be in those days for women who are pregnant and for mothers with little babies! [18] Pray to God that these things will not happen in the winter! [19] For the trouble of those days will be far worse than any the world has ever known from the very beginning when God created the world until the present time. Nor will there ever be anything like it again. [20] But the Lord has reduced the number of those days; if he had not, nobody would survive. For the sake of his chosen people, however, he has reduced those days.

[21] "Then, if anyone says to you, 'Look, here is the Messiah!' or, 'Look, there he is!' — do not believe him. [22] For false Messiahs and false prophets will appear. They will perform miracles and wonders in order to deceive even God's chosen people, if possible. [23] Be on your guard! I have told you everything before the time comes.

The Coming of the Son of Man
(Mt 24.29–31; Lk 21.25–28)

[24] "In the days after that time of trouble the sun will grow dark, the moon will no longer shine, [25] the stars will fall from heaven, and the powers in space will be driven from their courses. [26] Then the Son of Man will appear, coming in the clouds with great power and glory. [27] He will send the angels out to the four corners of the earth to gather God's chosen people from one end of the world to the other.

The Lesson of the Fig Tree
(Mt 24.32–35; Lk 21.29–33)

[28] "Let the fig tree teach you a lesson. When its branches become green and tender and it starts putting out leaves, you know that summer is near. [29] In the same way, when you see these things happening, you will know that the time is near, ready to begin. [a] [30] Remember that all these things will happen before the people now living have all died. [31] Heaven and earth will pass away, but my words will never pass away.

a **13.29** the time is near, ready to begin; *or* he is near, ready to come.

No one Knows the Day or Hour
(Mt 24.36–44)

³² "No one knows, however, when that day or hour will come — neither the angels in heaven, nor the Son; only the Father knows. ³³ Be on watch, be alert, for you do not know when the time will come. ³⁴ It will be like a man who goes away from home on a journey and leaves his servants in charge, after giving to each one his own work to do and after telling the doorkeeper to keep watch. ³⁵ Be on guard, then, because you do not know when the master of the house is coming — it might be in the evening or at midnight or before dawn or at sunrise. ³⁶ If he comes suddenly, he must not find you asleep. ³⁷ What I say to you, then, I say to all: watch!"

The Plot against Jesus
(Mt 26.1–5; Lk 22.1–2; Jn 11.45–53)

14 It was now two days before the Festival of Passover and Unleavened Bread. The chief priests and the teachers of the Law were looking for a way to arrest Jesus secretly and put him to death. ² "We must not do it during the festival," they said, "or the people might riot."

Jesus is Anointed at Bethany
(Mt 26.6–13; Jn 12.1–8)

³ Jesus was in Bethany at the house of Simon, a man who had suffered from a dreaded skin disease. While Jesus was eating, a woman came in with an alabaster jar full of a very expensive perfume made of pure nard. She broke the jar and poured the perfume on Jesus' head. ⁴ Some of the people there became angry and said to one another, "What was the use of wasting the perfume? ⁵ It could have been sold for more than three hundred silver coins ᵃ and the money given to the poor!" And they criticized her harshly.

⁶ But Jesus said, "Leave her alone! Why are you bothering her? She has done a fine and beautiful thing for me. ⁷ You will always have poor people with you, and any time you want to, you can help them. But you will not always have me. ⁸ She did what she could; she poured perfume on my body to prepare it ahead of time for burial. ⁹ Now, I assure

ᵃ **14.5** SILVER COINS: *See 6.37.*

you that wherever the gospel is preached all over the world, what she has done will be told in memory of her."

Judas Agrees to Betray Jesus
(Mt 26.14–16; Lk 22.3–6)

¹⁰ Then Judas Iscariot, one of the twelve disciples, went off to the chief priests in order to betray Jesus to them. ¹¹ They were pleased to hear what he had to say, and promised to give him money. So Judas started looking for a good chance to hand Jesus over to them.

Jesus Eats the Passover Meal with his Disciples
(Mt 26.17–25; Lk 22.7–14, 21–23; Jn 13.21–30)

¹² On the first day of the Festival of Unleavened Bread, the day the lambs for the Passover meal were killed, Jesus' disciples asked him, "Where do you want us to go and get the Passover meal ready for you?"

¹³ Then Jesus sent two of them with these instructions: "Go into the city, and a man carrying a jar of water will meet you. Follow him ¹⁴ to the house he enters, and say to the owner of the house: 'The Teacher says, Where is the room where my disciples and I will eat the Passover meal?' ¹⁵ Then he will show you a large upstairs room, prepared and furnished, where you will get everything ready for us."

¹⁶ The disciples left, went to the city, and found everything just as Jesus had told them; and they prepared the Passover meal.

¹⁷ When it was evening, Jesus came with the twelve disciples. ¹⁸ While they were at the table eating, Jesus said, "I tell you that one of you will betray me — one who is eating with me."

¹⁹ The disciples were upset and began to ask him, one after the other, "Surely you don't mean me, do you?"

²⁰ Jesus answered, "It will be one of you twelve, one who dips his bread in the dish with me. ²¹ The Son of Man will die as the Scriptures say he will; but how terrible for that man who betrays the Son of Man! It would have been better for that man if he had never been born!"

This is my body (14.22)

The Lord's Supper
(Mt 26.26–30; Lk 22.14–20; 1 Cor. 11.23–25)

22 While they were eating, Jesus took a piece of bread, gave a prayer of thanks, broke it, and gave it to his disciples. "Take it," he said, "this is my body."

23 Then he took a cup, gave thanks to God, and handed it to them; and they all drank from it. 24 Jesus said, "This is my blood which is poured out for many, my blood which seals God's covenant. 25 I tell you, I will never again drink this wine until the day I drink the new wine in the Kingdom of God."

26 Then they sang a hymn and went out to the Mount of Olives.

Jesus Predicts Peter's Denial
(Mt 26.31–35; Lk 22.31–34; Jn 13.36–38)

27 Jesus said to them, "All of you will run away and leave me, for the scripture says, 'God will kill the shepherd, and the sheep will all be scattered.' 28 But after I am raised to life, I will go to Galilee ahead of you."

29 Peter answered, "I will never leave you, even though all the rest do!"

30 Jesus said to Peter, "I tell you that before the cock crows twice tonight, you will say three times that you do not know me."

³¹ Peter answered even more strongly, "I will never say that, even if I have to die with you!"

And all the other disciples said the same thing.

Jesus Prays in Gethsemane
(Mt 26.36–46; Lk 22.39–46)

³² They came to a place called Gethsemane, and Jesus said to his disciples, "Sit here while I pray." ³³ He took Peter, James, and John with him. Distress and anguish came over him, ³⁴ and he said to them, "The sorrow in my heart is so great that it almost crushes me. Stay here and keep watch."

³⁵ He went a little farther on, threw himself on the ground, and prayed that, if possible, he might not have to go through that time of suffering. ³⁶ "Father," he prayed, "my Father! All things are possible for you. Take this cup of suffering away from me. Yet not what I want, but what you want."

³⁷ Then he returned and found the three disciples asleep. He said to Peter, "Simon, are you asleep? Weren't you able to stay awake even for one hour?" ³⁸ And he said to them, "Keep watch, and pray that you will not fall into temptation. The spirit is willing, but the flesh is weak."

³⁹ He went away once more and prayed, saying the same words. ⁴⁰ Then he came back to the disciples and found them asleep; they could not keep their eyes open. And they did not know what to say to him.

⁴¹ When he came back the third time, he said to them, "Are you still sleeping and resting? Enough! The hour has come! Look, the Son of Man is now being handed over to the power of sinners. ⁴² Get up, let us go. Look, here is the man who is betraying me!"

The Arrest of Jesus
(Mt 26.47–56; Lk 22.47–53; Jn 18.3–12)

⁴³ Jesus was still speaking when Judas, one of the twelve disciples, arrived. With him was a crowd armed with swords and clubs, and sent by the chief priests, the teachers of the Law, and the elders. ⁴⁴ The traitor had given the crowd a signal: "The man I kiss is the one you want. Arrest him and take him away under guard."

So they arrested Jesus and held him tight   (14.46)

⁴⁵ As soon as Judas arrived, he went up to Jesus and said, "Teacher!" and kissed him. ⁴⁶ So they arrested Jesus and held him tight. ⁴⁷ But one of those standing there drew his sword and struck at the High Priest's slave, cutting off his ear. ⁴⁸ Then Jesus spoke up and said to them, "Did you have to come with swords and clubs to capture me, as though I were an outlaw? ⁴⁹ Day after day I was with you teaching in the Temple, and you did not arrest me. But the Scriptures must come true."

⁵⁰ Then all the disciples left him and ran away.

⁵¹ A certain young man, dressed only in a linen cloth, was following Jesus. They tried to arrest him, ⁵² but he ran away naked, leaving the cloth behind.

Jesus before the Council
(Mt 26.57–68; Lk 22.54–55, 63–71; Jn 18.13–14, 19–24)

⁵³ Then Jesus was taken to the High Priest's house, where all the chief priests, the elders, and the teachers of the Law were gathering. ⁵⁴ Peter followed from a distance and went into the courtyard of the High Priest's house. There he sat down with the guards, keeping himself warm by the fire. ⁵⁵ The chief priests and the whole Council tried to find some

evidence against Jesus in order to put him to death, but they could not find any. ⁵⁶ Many witnesses told lies against Jesus, but their stories did not agree.

⁵⁷ Then some men stood up and told this lie against Jesus: ⁵⁸ "We heard him say, 'I will tear down this Temple which men have made, and after three days I will build one that is not made by men.' " ⁵⁹ Not even they, however, could make their stories agree.

⁶⁰ The High Priest stood up in front of them all and questioned Jesus, "Have you no answer to the accusation they bring against you?"

⁶¹ But Jesus kept quiet and would not say a word. Again the High Priest questioned him, "Are you the Messiah, the Son of the Blessed God?"

⁶² "I am," answered Jesus, "and you will all see the Son of Man seated on the right of the Almighty and coming with the clouds of heaven!"

⁶³ The High Priest tore his robes and said, "We don't need any more witnesses! ⁶⁴ You heard his blasphemy. What is your decision?"

They all voted against him: he was guilty and should be put to death.

⁶⁵ Some of them began to spit on Jesus, and they blindfolded him and hit him. "Guess who hit you!" they said. And the guards took him and slapped him.

Peter Denies Jesus
(Mt 26.69–75; Lk 22.56–62; Jn 18.15–18, 25–27)

⁶⁶ Peter was still down in the courtyard when one of the High Priest's servant women came by. ⁶⁷ When she saw Peter warming himself, she looked straight at him and said, "You, too, were with Jesus of Nazareth."

⁶⁸ But he denied it. "I don't know . . . I don't understand what you are talking about," he answered, and went out into the passage. Just then a cock crowed. ᵃ

⁶⁹ The servant woman saw him there and began to repeat to the bystanders, "He is one of them!" ⁷⁰ But Peter denied it again.

a **14.68** *Some manuscripts do not have* Just then a cock crowed.

A cock crowed . . . and Peter remembered (14.72)

A little while later the bystanders accused Peter again, "You can't deny that you are one of them, because you, too, are from Galilee."

⁷¹ Then Peter said, "I swear that I am telling the truth! May God punish me if I am not! I do not know the man you are talking about!"

⁷² Just then a cock crowed a second time, and Peter remembered how Jesus had said to him, "Before the cock crows twice, you will say three times that you do not know me." And he broke down and cried.

Jesus is Brought before Pilate
(Mt 27.1–2, 11–14; Lk 23.1–5; Jn 18.28–38)

15 Early in the morning the chief priests met hurriedly with the elders, the teachers of the Law, and the whole Council, and made their plans. They put Jesus in chains, led him away, and handed him over to Pilate. ² Pilate questioned him, "Are you the king of the Jews?"

Jesus answered, "So you say."

³ The chief priests were accusing Jesus of many things, ⁴ so Pilate questioned him again, "Aren't you going to answer? Listen to all their accusations!"

⁵ Again Jesus refused to say a word, and Pilate was amazed.

Jesus is Sentenced to Death
(Mt 27.15–26; Lk 23.13–25; Jn 18.39—19.16)

⁶At every Passover Festival Pilate was in the habit of setting free any one prisoner the people asked for. ⁷At that time a man named Barabbas was in prison with the rebels who had committed murder in the riot. ⁸When the crowd gathered and began to ask Pilate for the usual favour, ⁹he asked them, "Do you want me to set free for you the king of the Jews?" ¹⁰He knew very well that the chief priests had handed Jesus over to him because they were jealous.

¹¹But the chief priests stirred up the crowd to ask, instead, for Pilate to set Barabbas free for them. ¹²Pilate spoke again to the crowd, "What, then, do you want me to do with the one you call the king of the Jews?"

¹³They shouted back, "Crucify him!"

¹⁴"But what crime has he committed?" Pilate asked.

They shouted all the louder, "Crucify him!"

¹⁵Pilate wanted to please the crowd, so he set Barabbas free for them. Then he had Jesus whipped and handed him over to be crucified.

The Soldiers Mock Jesus
(Mt 27.27–31; Jn 19.2–3)

¹⁶The soldiers took Jesus inside to the courtyard of the governor's palace and called together the rest of the company. ¹⁷They put a purple robe on Jesus, made a crown out of thorny branches, and put it on his head. ¹⁸Then they began to salute him: "Long live the King of the Jews!" ¹⁹They beat him over the head with a stick, spat on him, fell on their knees, and bowed down to him. ²⁰When they had finished mocking him, they took off the purple robe and put his own clothes back on him. Then they led him out to crucify him.

Jesus is Crucified
(Mt 27.32–44; Lk 23.26–43; Jn 19.17–27)

²¹On the way they met a man named Simon, who was coming into the city from the country, and the soldiers forced him to carry Jesus' cross. (Simon was from Cyrene and was the father of Alexander and Rufus.) ²²They took

Jesus to a place called Golgotha, which means "The Place of the Skull". ²³ There they tried to give him wine mixed with a drug called myrrh, but Jesus would not drink it. ²⁴ Then they crucified him and divided his clothes among themselves, throwing dice to see who would get which piece of clothing. ²⁵ It was nine o'clock in the morning when they crucified him. ²⁶ The notice of the accusation against him said: "The King of the Jews". ²⁷ They also crucified two bandits with Jesus, one on his right and the other on his left. ᵃ

Throwing dice   (15.24)

²⁹ People passing by shook their heads and hurled insults at Jesus: "Aha! You were going to tear down the Temple and build it up again in three days! ³⁰ Now come down from the cross and save yourself!"

³¹ In the same way the chief priests and the teachers of the Law jeered at Jesus, saying to each other, "He saved

a **15.27** *Some manuscripts add verse 28:* In this way the scripture came true which says, "He shared the fate of criminals" *(see Lk 22.37).*

Aha! . . . come down from the cross (15.29,30)

others, but he cannot save himself! ³²Let us see the Messiah, the king of Israel, come down from the cross now, and we will believe in him!"

And the two who were crucified with Jesus insulted him also.

The Death of Jesus
(Mt 27.45–56; Lk 23.44–49; Jn 19.28–30)

³³At noon the whole country was covered with darkness, which lasted for three hours. ³⁴At three o'clock Jesus cried out with a loud shout, *"Eloi, Eloi, lema sabachthani?"* which means, "My God, my God, why did you abandon me?"

³⁵Some of the people there heard him and said, "Listen, he is calling for Elijah!" ³⁶One of them ran up with a sponge, soaked it in cheap wine, and put it on the end of a stick. Then he held it up to Jesus' lips and said, "Wait! Let us see if Elijah is coming to bring him down from the cross!"

³⁷With a loud cry Jesus died.

³⁸ The curtain hanging in the Temple was torn in two, from top to bottom. ³⁹ The army officer who was standing there in front of the cross saw how Jesus had died. ^a "This man was really the Son of God!" he said.

⁴⁰ Some women were there, looking on from a distance. Among them were Mary Magdalene, Mary the mother of the younger James and of Joseph, and Salome. ⁴¹ They had followed Jesus while he was in Galilee and had helped him. Many other women who had come to Jerusalem with him were there also.

The Burial of Jesus
(Mt 27.57–61; Lk 23.50–56; Jn 19.38–42)

⁴²⁻⁴³ It was towards evening when Joseph of Arimathea arrived. He was a respected member of the Council, who was waiting for the coming of the Kingdom of God. It was Preparation day (that is, the day before the Sabbath), so Joseph went boldly into the presence of Pilate and asked him for the body of Jesus. ⁴⁴ Pilate was surprised to hear that Jesus was already dead. He called the army officer and asked him if Jesus had been dead a long time. ⁴⁵ After hearing the officer's report, Pilate told Joseph he could have the body. ⁴⁶ Joseph bought a linen sheet, took the body down, wrapped it in the sheet, and placed it in a tomb which had been dug out of solid rock. Then he rolled a large stone across the entrance to the tomb. ⁴⁷ Mary Magdalene and Mary the mother of Joseph were watching and saw where the body of Jesus was placed.

The Resurrection
(Mt 28.1–8; Lk 24.1–12; Jn 20.1–10)

16 After the Sabbath was over, Mary Magdalene, Mary the mother of James, and Salome bought spices to go and anoint the body of Jesus. ² Very early on Sunday morning, at sunrise, they went to the tomb. ³⁻⁴ On the way they said to one another, "Who will roll away the stone for us from the entrance to the tomb?" (It was a very large stone.) Then they looked up and saw that the stone had already been rolled back. ⁵ So they entered the tomb,

a **15.39** had died; *some manuscripts have* had cried out and died.

where they saw a young man sitting on the right, wearing a white robe — and they were alarmed.

⁶ "Don't be alarmed," he said. "I know you are looking for Jesus of Nazareth, who was crucified. He is not here — he has been raised! Look, here is the place where they put him. ⁷ Now go and give this message to his disciples, including Peter: 'He is going to Galilee ahead of you; there you will see him, just as he told you.' "

⁸ So they went out and ran from the tomb, distressed and terrified. They said nothing to anyone, because they were afraid.

So they went out and ran   (16.8)

AN OLD ENDING TO THE GOSPEL ᵃ
16.9–20

Jesus Appears to Mary Magdalene
(Mt 28.9–10; Jn 20.11–18)

[⁹ After Jesus rose from death early on Sunday, he appeared first to Mary Magdalene, from whom he had driven out seven demons. ¹⁰ She went and told his companions. They were mourning and crying; ¹¹ and when they heard her say that Jesus was alive and that she had seen him, they did not believe her.

a **16.9-20 heading** *Some manuscripts and ancient translations do not have this ending to the Gospel (verses 9–20).*

Jesus Appears to Two Disciples
(Lk 24.13–35)

¹²After this, Jesus appeared in a different manner to two of them while they were on their way to the country. ¹³They returned and told the others, but they would not believe it.

Jesus Appears to the Eleven
(Mt 28.16–20; Lk 24.36–49; Jn 20.19–23; Acts 1.6–8)

¹⁴Last of all, Jesus appeared to the eleven disciples as they were eating. He scolded them, because they did not have faith and because they were too stubborn to believe those who had seen him alive. ¹⁵He said to them, "Go throughout the whole world and preach the gospel to the whole human race. ¹⁶Whoever believes and is baptized will be saved; whoever does not believe will be condemned. ¹⁷Believers will be given the power to perform miracles: they will drive out demons in my name; they will speak in strange tongues; ¹⁸if they pick up snakes or drink any poison, they will not be harmed; they will place their hands on sick people, who will get well."

Jesus is Taken Up to Heaven
(Lk 24.50–53; Acts 1.9–11)

¹⁹After the Lord Jesus had talked with them, he was taken up to heaven and sat at the right side of God. ²⁰The disciples went and preached everywhere, and the Lord worked with them and proved that their preaching was true by the miracles that were performed.]

ANOTHER OLD ENDING ᵃ
16.9–10

[⁹The women went to Peter and his friends and gave them a brief account of all they had been told. ¹⁰After this, Jesus himself sent out through his disciples from the east to the west the sacred and ever-living message of eternal salvation.]

a **16.9-10 heading** *Some manuscripts and ancient translations have this shorter ending to the Gospel in addition to the longer ending (verses 9–20).*

PALESTINE
IN THE TIME OF
JESUS

Sidon

Zarephath

Tyre

PHOENICIA

Caesarea
Philippi

ITUREA

ABILENE

TRACHONITIS

GALILEE

Chorazin

Capernaum ● ● Bethsaida

Cana

Tiberias

LAKE GALILEE

△ Mount
Carmel

Nazareth

Nain

Gadara

D
E
C
A
P
O
L
I
S

(THE TEN TOWNS)

Caesarea

Salim
● Aenon

MEDITERRANEAN SEA

Mount Gerizim △

Sychar

Gerasa

SAMARIA

River Jordan

Arimathea

Ephraim

PEREA

Emmaus

Jericho

Jerusalem ● Bethphage
● Bethany

JUDEA ● Qumran

Bethlehem

DEAD SEA

IDUMEA

0   20   40   60

Kilometres

56

JERUSALEM IN
NEW TESTAMENT TIMES

To Caesarea

Present City Wall

To Jericho

Damascus
Gate

Pool of
Bethzatha

PRAETORIUM

FORT

Ancient
City Wall

To Bethany

Gate

TEMPLE

Golgotha

Gate

Beautiful Gate

Gethsemane

Gate

To Joppa

Court of
Gentiles

Solomon's
Porch

Gennath
Gate

To Bethlehem

Bridge

Gates

HEROD'S
PALACE

Pool

Present City Wall

Pool of
Siloam

KIDRON VALLEY

0   200   400

Metres

Gate

Roads

V A L L E Y   O F   H I N N O M

To Dead
Sea

SOME STORIES FROM THE GOSPEL

SOME OF JESUS' PARABLES

SOME OF JESUS' MIRACLES

WHERE TO LOOK WHEN YOU ARE FEELING . . .